The Pharaohs of Ancient Egypt

Story by **Claire Derouin**
Text by **Viviane Koenig**
Activities by **Béatrice Garel**
Game by **Catherine Pauwels**

contents

Story
Pharaoh's Strange Dream — 4

Mega-infos
The Land Where It Never Rains — 12
The Old Kingdom — 14
Pharaoh Zoser and his Wise Imhotep — 16
Working in Stone — 18
The Great Pyramid of Khufu — 20

Activity
Build a Pyramid — 22

Mega-infos
On Foot or by Boat — 24
True Pharaohs or Minor Princes? — 26
The Middle Kingdom — 28
The Army and Fortresses — 30
Pharaoh's Peasants — 32

Activity
The Game of Senet — 34

Mega-infos
Pharaoh, the Best of Fishermen — 36
Foreigners Become Kings! — 38
The New Kingdom — 40

Anecdotes

Incredible but True!   42

Mega-infos

The Great Rameses II   44
A Village of Gifted
  Artisans   46

Game

The Artisans at Work   48

Mega-infos

The Learned Scientists   50
A Strange Era   52
The Persians and Greeks   54
End of Pharaohs   56

Quiz

True or False?   58

Index   62

Answers   63

Stickers

Picture Cards

Story

Pharaoh's Strange Dream

Claire Derouin

Dangerous Threats

It was a wasted morning. The gazelles were peacefully drinking at the edge of the Nile's blue waters. Scanning the empty horizon one last time, Egypt's young Pharaoh decided not to continue his hunt any longer. There were no lions anywhere to be seen. Mekhet Ra handed his bow to his bearer. The slave put it away in its red leather case. Together, they set off in the royal chariot in the direction of Memphis. As they passed a clump of papyrus reeds, a startled group of wild geese took to

4

Story

the air. Pharaoh watched, perplexed, as they fled.

"What I wouldn't give to see the Libyan bandits, who are ravaging my western border, clear off in the same way!" he thought.

A sense of weariness suddenly washed over him. The Libyans had been raiding for more than 1,000 years. Finally, they had been driven off by his father, the old Pharaoh—may he live with the Gods! But no sooner had young Pharaoh assumed the Double Crown of the Two Egypts than the bandits had resumed their attacks. For more than four months, his army had been trying to drive them off. But neither his charioteers nor his infantrymen had succeeded! Not even the famous royal archers had been able to stop them.

"Each day, Egypt is sinking a little further into chaos," the young monarch said to himself. "Disorder has replaced the just rule of the Gods. I am incapable of keeping the peace in my own kingdom. My mission as Pharaoh is failing!"

This confession made him shiver with terror. His heart began to race. Struck by a sudden dizzy spell, he pulled clumsily on the reins. The chariot stood still in the bright sunlight. The young Pharaoh dismounted. He staggered toward the shade of a nearby boulder, his worried slave at his side, and sat down heavily.

Story

Hardly had Pharaoh sat down, when a great weariness overcame him. His eyelids closed and he fell into a deep sleep. His slave stood over him in terror.

A Message from the Gods

Within an hour, the spell passed. Pharaoh awakened. He set off for the palace and immediately summoned his senior magicians. Dressed in their long, white robes, the three men—high priest Rai, Pasar the astronomer, and the young wonder, Oubaoney—proceeded at a dignified pace to the Council Chamber. Their lord was waiting for them, sitting on his throne and looking very serious.

"His Divine Majesty requires our services?" the three honored sages asked respectfully.

Pharaoh signaled to them to sit down and told them the details of the strange dream he had had while sleeping under the rock.

"I saw a great storm striking Egypt!" he explained in a voice trembling with emotion. "A sea of sand engulfed my palace in the space of a few heartbeats! When I thought the sky was clearing, a huge whirlwind came out of the western desert, heading straight for me. It was so powerful that it dug an enormous crater in the middle of the dunes beside me. Then, in a deafening roar, the

Story

wind changed. The sand shot straight up into the air to form a gleaming, golden bridge. It stretched from the earth to the blood red sun, which roared like an angry lion."

The sages looked at each other in silence. There were certainly omens of the future hidden in such a dream!

"Rai, you were my teacher," Pharaoh continued. "It was you who told me the great truth that some dreams are messages sent from the Gods. But how am I to tell the divine dreams from the ordinary? This storm terrifies me! It makes me think of the attacks by the Libyans. I fear that this dream foretells a terrible invasion."

"Perhaps the *Book of Dreams* will help us to understand exactly what the Gods meant," suggested Rai.

"Go and get it, my friend!" said Pharaoh. "These are serious times!"

The Book of Dreams

"Let us see what the scroll says about your dream, Your Majesty," began Rai. He unrolled the long sheet of papyrus covered with colored hieroglyphics. All gathered around to look at the pictures.

"Here is the first question," said Pasar. "Before the storm came, had His Majesty dreamed of eating cucumbers?"

"Cucumbers? What a strange idea! No, I hadn't eaten any cucumbers."

"Good," said Pasar. "We can therefore eliminate the possibility of a dispute with the king of Hatti."

"When His Majesty speaks of the roaring by the sun, might it not have been more like the yowling of a cat?" asked Oubaoney.

"Certainly not!" replied Pharaoh. "Do you think I don't know the difference between a lion and a cat?"

"That's what I feared," said Oubaoney. "The sender of this dream must be the great Ra, God of the Sun whose flames can devour flesh as quickly as the teeth of a lion. To go red like this, I am afraid that he has been angered."

"But why?" asked Pharaoh. "Every day I perform the required services to renew the power of the Gods on Earth. And have I not built great temples in Their honor?

"Your Majesty, may we continue!" said Rai. "One last question: from which direction did the sand come?"

"From the southwest, without any doubt," replied Pharaoh.

"Hmm!" said the sage, shaking his head. "Your bad feeling is confirmed. It seems as if Ra has decided to let Egypt be invaded by the Libyans. We must assume that he is angry, as Oubaoney suggests. We are getting

somewhere! But we still have to find the reason for His wrath, so we can calm Him before it is too late."

"I've got an idea!" exclaimed Pasar. "What if the crater formed by the whirlwind was a sign to show us that it was an important site—the location of a buried monument, for example?"

"Why not!" exclaimed Pharaoh. "It's true that the Gods can't bear it when their temples and statues are poorly maintained. The dream could be a warning of what will happen unless we do something. Let's go and examine that site!"

The Secret of the Dunes

On seeing the rock where Pharaoh had slept, the magicians suspected immediately that it was the tip of an important monument.

"It's a pyramid!" asserted Pasar, very sure of himself.

"You haven't a clue," said Oubaoney indignantly. "This rounded shape could only belong to a temple."

"Enough of this," cried Pharaoh. "Call for laborers!" And he himself began to dig. Even Pharaoh will wield a spade for his father, the great God Ra!

Five hundred workmen were brought up to relieve Pharaoh. After three days and nights of relentless work,

Story

a gigantic head at last emerged from the sand. Its huge eyes glowed in the rays of the setting sun. And its smiling lips seemed to give out a message of love to the entire kingdom!

In the following days, the statue's body was in turn uncovered. Pharaoh had been called back to the palace on business. When he returned, the excavation was complete. As the workmen laid down their tools, Pharaoh let out a cry of amazement.

"It's a Sphinx! Ra's protection is restored!" He turned to Pasar. "Is it on the Sphinx list in the *Book of Guardians*?"

Pasar's eyes gleamed with joy as he answered. "Divine Majesty, no. This one was made and lost in the sand before the Book was written. It must be over 2,000 years old. A great guardian of olden days has been returned to us!" He turned to the other people gathered round.

"All praise to his Divine Majesty. May He live forever!"

Pharaoh spoke at the foot of the statue.

"My children, Father Ra has given us the sign. I shall go west and south to destroy the Libyans. I leave this instant! Glorious victory awaits!" And he mounted his chariot and drove off.

Story

Ra then showed his favor, indeed. Before Pharaoh even arrived at the front, his armies had broken up the enemy's main border camp. To avenge this bitter defeat, the Libyan king himself came out to challenge Pharaoh. In hand-to-hand combat, the Son of Ra defeated the Libyan, who was held as hostage for his countrymen's good behavior.

The grateful Mekhet Ra employed thirty men from his personal guard for the daily upkeep of the Sphinx. And he ordered a stone tablet to be placed at the foot of the statue. On it, the great adventure that brought peace to his kingdoms and glory to his reign was engraved for the future generations.

Mega-infos

It Never Rains

■ In the Heart of the Desert
It is a land of mountains and dunes. Sand blows everywhere. In the Egyptian desert not a blade of grass can be found. A narrow green valley runs the length of the Nile River. Source of all life in Egypt, the Nile has a wonderful habit. Every year it floods its valley for three months before returning to its natural course.

■ In Unity There Is Strength
Farming in the Nile Valley required the cooperation of many people to build canals for flood control. Leaders appeared, each more powerful than the last. More than 5,000 years ago, the southern king conquered the north. Egypt, the double kingdom, had been born.

■ Pharaoh
Used for over a thousand years before the birth of Christ, the word *Pharaoh* comes from the Egyptian word for "great house." Referring first to the palace itself, the word came to mean "he who is master of it."

■ Organizing, Always Organizing
Owner of all the land, Pharaoh ruled absolutely from his palace at Memphis, the first capital of Egypt. His priests, soldiers, artisans, and peasants all worked to advance his glory. And his scribes wrote everything down.

Map: LOWER EGYPT — Giza, Saqqara, Memphis; UPPER EGYPT — Valley of the Kings, Abydos, Thebes, Deir al-Bahari, Deir al-Medina; Abu Simbel; NUBIA; KUSH; Nile River

| 580 | NEW KINGDOM | -1085 | -332 | Greek Period | -30 | Roman Period |

enhotep — Thutmosis — Ramses — Alexander the Great — Cleopatra

Mega-infos

The Old

Founded about 2800 B.C., the Old Kingdom lasted for five centuries. It was the time of the great pyramids.

■ Hundreds of Civil Servants
Hundreds of scribes carried out Pharaoh's orders and wrote down important information. Written on papyrus, on scraps of pottery, or on stone tablets, messages were quickly delivered on the boats that constantly sailed the river.

■ Writing, an Absolute Necessity
Early on, the Egyptians invented two kinds of writing: the complicated *hieroglyphs* for monuments and state documents, and the simpler *hieratic script* for everyday use. In the temples and the royal palace, privileged young men learned how to read, write, and calculate. Even the princes had to learn.

14

Mega-infos

Kingdom

■ What Are Hieroglyphs?

Hieroglyphs are pictures that express things, ideas, and sounds. A circle can represent the sun, but it can also mean light, or the passing of time. A picture of a mouth means just that, but also stands for the sound "re." Pictures can be com-bined to form long words. To make things even more difficult, hieroglyphs can be read from left to right, right to left, or top to bottom. And the words are never separated from each other!

■ Thousands of Texts

Scribes, "with their smooth limbs and soft hands," were in charge of all the country's affairs. Nothing was outside their control, and they paid no taxes. Their profession was the most important of all callings, because only they could read and write. They recorded everything—the amount of grain harvested; the number of inhabitants in the villages; the height of the flood; the size of the stones to be transported; the amount of gold brought back from an expedition...

A scribe's writing materials.

Mega-infos

Pharaoh Zoser and

4700 years ago Pharaoh Zoser dreamed of a gigantic tomb, and his dream became reality.

■ The Ingenious Imhotep

Zoser was lucky to have at his side Imhotep, his gifted *vizier*, who was also an architect, priest, doctor, and scribe. Imhotep worked for years to fulfill his Pharaoh's desire. At the end, the greatest structure of the age stood under the sun at Saqqara.

❦ *Vizir*
The vizier fulfilled the functions of the prime minister. He was the "ears, eyes, and hands" of the king.

Mega-infos

is Wise Imhotep

■ A Stepped Pyramid
Almost 200 feet (61 meters) high, and originally covered with blocks of fine limestone, Zoser's tomb with its giant steps resembles a staircase mounting to the heavens. Would the soul of Pharaoh climb those steps to rejoin the Gods on the day of his death?

■ A Well-Guarded Tomb
Enclosed by a high wall, almost a mile (1.6 kilometers) in circumference, courts, chapels, and other buildings surround the pyramid. Above this encircling wall, proud and menacing, are dozens of carved stone cobras, hoods spread, guarding the compound from the menace of the desert. But if you look closely, you will see something strange. To confuse evil spirits and would-be grave robbers, the wall has fourteen false doors, and only one real one!

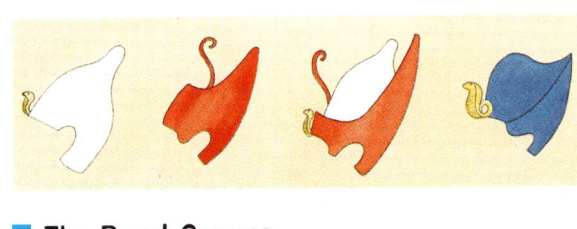

■ The Royal Crowns
As a symbol of Egyptian unity, Pharaoh wore a double crown. It combined the white serpent crown of Upper (southern) Egypt and the red crown of Lower (northern) Egypt, which had originally been made of woven reeds. In the New Kingdom (1580 to 1085 B.C.) the crown worn by Pharaoh was often blue.

17

Mega-infos

Working in Stone

Under the blazing sun, enormous blocks of fine stone were cut from the sides of mountains at the royal quarries.

Cutting Blocks

Workers drilled holes using bow drills and sand. Then they drove dry, wooden wedges into the holes with mallets. Soaked in water, the wedges swelled, splitting the stone and detaching it from the quarry wall. Then the blocks, some weighing many tons, were levered onto a sledge for transport. The largest blocks were moved on log rollers.

Mega-infos

■ An Army of Workers

Yellow sandstone, white limestone, pink granite—the blocks were sometimes pulled along by oxen, but more often by men. Tomb paintings show lines of as many as 200 men pulling gigantic statues.

■ Dragging the Sledge over the Sand

An overseer yells out brief orders. A worker gives rhythm to the work by beating a drum. Another throws water onto the ground so that the sledge does not catch fire because of the heat of friction. A guard strikes the workers who are too slow. After days of effort under the blazing sun, the stone arrives at the banks of the great river.

■ Floating on the Nile

With skill and care, the men load the stones onto the boats. They prefer the flood season, when the Nile majestically spreads out, because the difficult journey over land is that much shorter.

■ More Hauling

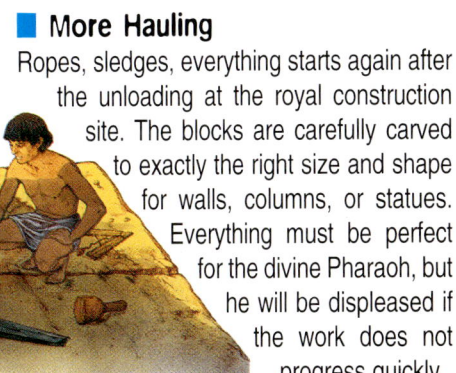

Ropes, sledges, everything starts again after the unloading at the royal construction site. The blocks are carefully carved to exactly the right size and shape for walls, columns, or statues. Everything must be perfect for the divine Pharaoh, but he will be displeased if the work does not progress quickly.

19

Mega-infos

The Great Pyramid of Khufu

Around 2700 B.C., the great pyramid of Pharaoh Khufu (also called Cheops) was completed. The pyramid itself, one ivory statuette, and some stories—this is all that remains of this great king's magnificent tomb.

■ Khufu and his Pyramid

Today, the Great Pyramid is 450 feet (137 meters) high. Its missing point added another 33 feet (10 meters). The four steep sides were covered with white limestone—also long gone. At the heart of this structure, corridors lead to the royal chamber. There, the mummy of Pharaoh was placed on the day of his burial.

Mega-infos

■ The Treasures Hidden in the Pyramid

Khufu's mummy, his treasures, the offerings of food, tools, and other objects originally placed within the pyramid were carried off by grave robbers thousands of years ago. All that remains is a mysterious granite *sarcophagus*, without ornament or inscription.

> ❣ **Sarcophagus**
> *A massive stone box in which Pharaoh's coffin was placed.*

■ Khufu and his Temples

A great road, paved in stone, descends from the pyramid plateau towards another group of temples in the nearby valley. Offerings and prayers, thought to be necessary for the comfort of Pharaoh in the "next world," continued long after his death.

Over the centuries, the tombs of the Pharaohs were often robbed.

■ Khufu and his Royal Barges

The Egyptians believed that each day Ra, the Great Sun God, sailed across the sky in a celestial boat. So that Pharaoh could sail with Ra, great ditches were dug at the foot of the pyramid. Dismantled "solar barges," complete with ropes and oars, were hidden there. Quite a puzzle! Reconstructed several years ago, the largest of these barges was 75 feet (23 meters) long!

Activity

Build a

In the Old Kingdom the Egyptians erected fantastic monuments to the glory of their Pharaohs: the pyramids. The shape of the pyramid pointed towards the heavens, where Pharaoh would sit with the Sun God Ra.

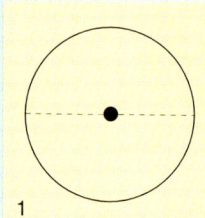
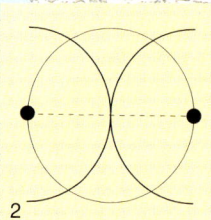
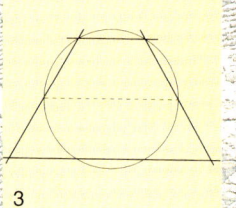
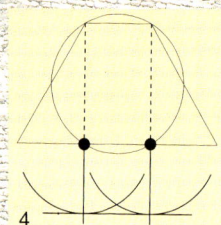

You will need:
- a sheet of construction paper
- a compass
- scissors
- tape or glue
- a ruler

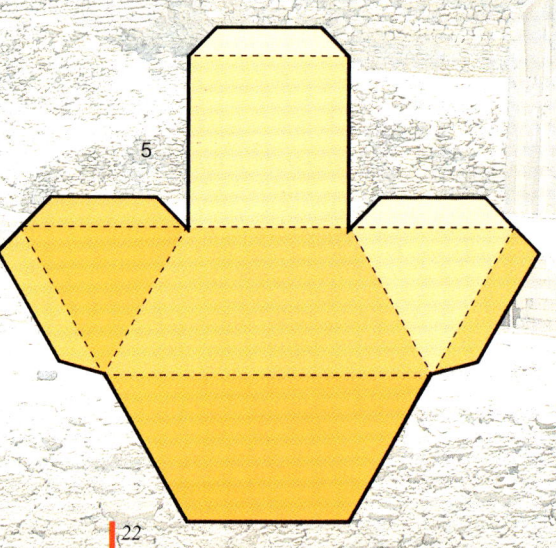

Pyramid

Activity

1. Follow the illustrated steps 1, 2, 3, 4 (on the opposite page) to mark the paper. Use a compass set for radius of 3 inches (7.6 centimeters).

2. Sketch in the folding tabs as shown in picture.

3. Fold along the dotted lines.

4. Glue or tape the flaps.

5. Make another, the same as the first.

Solution on page 63.

On Foot or by Boat

In the Old Kingdom, Egyptians went everywhere on foot or by boat, using their donkeys only to carry loads. They constructed their boats of wood and bundles of papyrus reeds.

■ Pharaoh Never Walked

Over short distances, Pharaoh was carried in a *sedan* chair. This was a throne mounted on long poles, which servants carried on their shoulders. Other servants waved long plumes of ostrich feathers, carried the royal sandals, or perhaps a silver pitcher full of cool water. Pharaoh himself held on to his precious fly swatter!

Mega-infos

■ Barges Fit for the King

Constructed by skilled carpenters, the hulls of the royal vessels were made from planks of wood coated with resin on the inside. The sails were hung from one or two masts. A tiller at the back, and two banks of oars on each side, kept the royal barge on course. If the wind dropped, the rowers began to work. Pharaoh must not be delayed!

■ Pleasant Voyages for Pharaoh

A little tent of fine material was installed on the deck. With armchairs, footstools, jars of cool water, and delicious cakes, Pharaoh and his family were very comfortable. Protected from the sun and prying eyes, they reached their destination relaxed and refreshed.

Mega-infos

True Pharaohs

The end of the Old Kingdom was a time of great troubles. A scribe wrote: "The country is upside down. Laughter has vanished."

■ **To the Attack!**
From 2260 B.C., the successors of Pharaoh Pepi II tried to keep control of an unsettled country. The nobles in the provinces wanted to be kings themselves. The people rebelled. A violent revolution broke out. Fear reigned. Bandits roamed the countryside.

Mega-infos

or Minor Princes?

■ The End of the Old Kingdom
"Seventy Pharaohs in seventy days!," it was murmured in the old capital. The situation kept getting worse. Soon, there were three kingdoms: the north-east was in the hands of Asian invaders. There was a Pharaoh in the central city of Herakleopolis, and another in the south, at Thebes.

■ The Time of the Prince Kings
The kingdom was broken. Only minor princes remained. Neither powerful nor rich, each dreamed of becoming Pharaoh. Instead, they settled for modest palaces and tombs dug out of the mountains in the desert. "Who will unite us? When will our Pharaoh return?" the people wondered. It would be a prince of Thebes, Intef, who fulfilled their hopes.

■ Some Clever Artists
In these troubled times, fine granite, alabaster, gold, and precious stones were not available to the artists. To please the princes in their palaces, the Gods in their temples, and the dead in their tombs, artists adapted. They worked in soft, cheap acacia and sycamore wood, and replaced the large stone statues with small, simple clay models.

Mega-infos

The Middle Kingdom

In 2050 B.C. Mentuhotep reunited Egypt. This was at the beginning of the Middle Kingdom, a period of great splendor that lasted more than two centuries.

■ The Return of Order

During his long reign, Mentuhotep I reconquered southern Nubia and made Thebes, a small provincial market town, the capital of his realm. Many of his successors, with impressive names like Amenemhet, and Senroset, were strong rulers, worthy of their ancestor. They enlarged the royal domains as far as Libya and Syria.

Boats came to Thebes filled with gold, ivory, ebony, strange beasts like monkeys and giraffes, rare perfumes, and other exotic treasures.

■ The Threat from Within

The Pharaohs tried to control the dangerously powerful nobles of the kingdom. Did not each dream of one day becoming Pharaoh himself? Senroset III divided Egypt into three regions and chose for each a *viceroy*—a governor who ruled in Pharaoh's name for a limited time only.

■ Deserts and Great Journeys

The glorious Pharaohs ordered incredible expeditions to far off lands in search of precious goods. Wells were dug along roads pushed into unexplored territories. Explorers searched for precious metals and gems. Naval expeditions down the east coast of Africa brought back gold, ivory, and slaves.

■ An Age of Wealth and Power

During the Middle Kingdom, the valley of the Nile was covered with glorious monuments. Long inscriptions celebrated the power of the Gods and Pharaohs. The great irrigation works of Amenemhet III are still in use today.

Mega-infos

The Army

The army spread fear of Pharaoh to foreign countries and maintained order throughout the realm.

■ Pharaoh, a Warrior Without Equal

"A brave man who operates with the force of his arm, a man of action without equal," said the Egyptians about Senroset I, a great Pharaoh of the Middle Kingdom. He must have looked magnificent as he reviewed his soldiers, the golden serpent *uraeus* gleaming from the crown on his head!

Uraeus
A cobra made of pure gold, mounted on the royal crown. It was said to spit magical fire on Pharaoh's enemies.

■ Good Soldiers

The disciplined soldiers of Pharaoh paraded in regular ranks behind their standard bearer, attacking their enemies, guarding expeditions into the burning deserts, watching over royal works. Armed with spears, slings, bows and arrows, clubs, axes, or daggers, they wore no armor, using only simple shields of wood and leather for protection.

30

Mega-infos

and Fortresses

■ Fortresses and Magic
To attack enemies was not enough, the kingdom must also be defended. Frontier fortresses were manned by tough soldiers, constantly on the alert. Magic was used as well. Priest-magicians made clay figures of enemies, which were smashed, burned, or buried in cursing ceremonies. Pharaoh could then sleep in peace.

Mega-infos

Pharaoh's Peasants

Always working, the Egyptians did not allow a single piece of land to go to waste. The precious fields were continually threatened by desert sands carried by the wind.

■ Sow in Mud, then Water . . .

From the moment the waters of the Nile retreated, the peasants worked the muddy soil with a plow pulled by oxen, or even with simple hoes. After sowing wheat, barley, or flax under the vigilant eye of the grain-scribe who supervised them, they let sheep roam in the fields. The seeds were pushed into the soft mud under their hooves. The peasants drew water from their carefully tended canals to irrigate their crops.

■ The Harvest

At harvest time the peasants, armed with sickles, cut the stalks to the rhythm of a flute-player. The sheaves were carried on donkeys to the threshing floor at the entrance to the village. Oxen, tied to a central post, trampled the harvest as they walked around in a circle. When the straw was broken off the grains, the mixture was swept up and thrown into the air. The chaff blew away, leaving clean grain behind.

■ Dangerous Animals

The great animals were both feared and worshipped. The hippopotamus, the crocodile, and the lion were all to be avoided. Clouds of crop-devouring locusts were also dreaded.

Mega-infos

The grain was sown.

The grain was separated from the chaff.

The scribe calculated the tax.

■ A Tax for Pharaoh

The scribes of the royal granaries measured the harvest and took a share as a tax for the upkeep of the state. What remained had to feed everyone until the next harvest. A portion was also set aside to make offerings to the Gods and the spirits of the dead. After the thanksgiving festivals, it was back to work for the peasants!

Water to irrigate the fields was raised with a shadouf, which was invented during the New Kingdom.

Activity

The Gam[e]

Some magnificent game boards have been found in Egyptian tombs. One, named *senet,* was the ancestor of backgammon. Colored pebbles or beads were used as playing pieces. You can make a senet from an egg carton and some beans.

 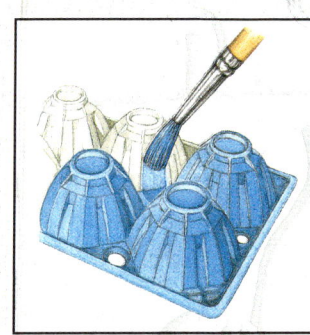

You will need:
- an empty carton for a dozen eggs
- 48 beans
- yellow, brown, and blue paint
- a brush
- scissors

1. Cut the cover off the egg carton.

2. Paint the inside yellow, the outside blue.

3. With a fine brush, paint brown and blue lines. Add Egypti[an] designs like those in the illustration.

# of Senet

Activity

The rules of the game

1. At the beginning of each game, each compartment contains four beans.

2. Taking turns, each player takes all the beans from any compartment on his side and places them one by one into neighboring compartments in a counterclockwise direction.

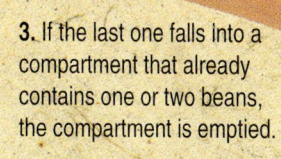

3. If the last one falls into a compartment that already contains one or two beans, the compartment is emptied.

4. The game ends when the loser has no more beans on his side.

Mega-infos

Pharaoh, the Best of Fishermen

In the marshes, Pharaohs hunted for pleasure, side by side with fishermen and herders. Dangerous animals abounded, and also, no doubt, the disturbed Gods of the swamps.

Mega-infos

■ The Skillful Fishermen
The Egyptians loved to eat fish—fresh, dried, or salted. Best of all, fish were free if you could catch them in the river or the canals. The most choice selections always went to the royal table. Almost naked in the sun, fishermen hurled harpoons and cast nets.

■ Royal Hunting
Sometimes, the fishermen spotted Pharaoh in his long barge, gliding through the reeds. The people stared as Pharaoh hunted. His club might hit a duck, or his harpoon pierce a fish with sparkling scales.

■ The Poor Herders
Living out in the open with their beasts for months on end, the herders cared for their flocks, dreaming of their village. They tended cattle, sheep, and goats. Always on guard against hyenas, jackals, and lions, they had to be swift and brave. In the vast swamps they faced other dangers, such as crocodiles, snakes, and scorpions. Hungry, dressed only in a scrap of cloth, the herders led hard lives.

■ Animals Were Wealth
The owners of the livestock were wealthy. Beasts were rented out to carry loads, pull the plows and sledges, and to thresh the grain. Herders and peasants rarely ate meat, but the nobles and Pharaoh had it often. As with the grain crop, scribes numbered the flocks—and Pharaoh always got his share.

Mega-infos

Foreigners Become Kings!

Confusion and decline came to the Middle Kingdom. There were forty Pharaohs in a single century. Then Egypt was invaded!

■ Foreigners Come to Conquer

Wandering herdsmen from Asia, known as the Hyksos, took advantage of the disorder in Egypt. They invaded, and with their new weapons they smashed the Egyptian armies. They had swift chariots and iron swords that cut through the bronze of the Egyptians. By about 1680 B.C. they had conquered the country.

■ The Horse Appears

Middle Kingdom nobles rode to war in carts pulled by donkeys. The Hyksos fought in swift, horse-drawn chariots, and could shoot their arrows or throw spears on the run.

■ Centuries of Anarchy

The Hyksos at first governed like bandits, stealing whatever they wanted and leaving a trail of ruin behind them. Eventually they settled down and established a harsh order, enforced by their troops. But life for the peasants changed little. They continued to work, watched over by scribes who collected the taxes as before.

Mega-infos

■ Egyptianization

Gradually, the Hyksos adopted Egyptian ways, but they never united the whole country under a single Pharaoh. A number of powerful lords governed small regions. They adopted the Egyptian language, customs, and religion. However, they never achieved the efficiently organized government of the native Egyptians. Conditions in the country remained chaotic.

Mega-infos

The New

About 1580 B.C., Ahmose, prince of Thebes, drove out the Hyksos and reunited the country. Thus began the New Kingdom, which endured for five hundred years.

Mega-infos

Kingdom

■ Great Victories!
Thebes became the capital of the realm and its god, Amen, took first place in the country. Ahmose and his successors of the eighteenth royal family, or *dynasty*, conquered vast territories. Tireless warriors, the four Amenohoteps and four Thutmoses expanded Egypt into a great empire. The conquered peoples offered rich tributes. Enormous monuments were built to proclaim Pharaoh's glory.

Thutmose

■ Grand Temples
"All our glory comes from Amen!" Thus thought the great Pharaohs. For this sun god, pictured as a human body with the head of a ram, a solar disk between his horns, they built gigantic temples. Magnificent offerings were made: weapons and vessels of gold and silver, lapis-lazuli and turquoise, finely carved statues, bales of cloth, baskets of food....

Amenhotep

■ The Valley of the Kings
The last pyramid had been built 1,000 years before. Near Thebes, the new Pharaohs chose for their burial ground a mountain that had the shape of a natural pyramid. The work lasted for centuries. Workers attacked the rock, making rooms and corridors. Carving, sculpting, and painting, they prepared everything needed for the everlasting life of Pharaoh in the next world.

■ The Tomb of "King Tut"
Tutankhamen, an undistinguished Pharaoh who reigned for less then ten years, owes his fame to the fact that his grave miraculously escaped robbers. His modest tomb in the Valley of the Kings yielded a treasure trove, including his famous gold mask inlaid with blue lapis-lazuli, brown agate, and colored glass.

Tutankhamen

Anecdotes

Incredible

● THE INVENTION OF INCOME TAX

Around 650 B.C. Pharaoh decided that each year, every Egyptian should report his wealth to a local official, who calculated the tax due. Tax evasion, or the making of a false report, was punished by death!

● STRANGE VASES

The Egyptian potters, who were gifted artisans, made some gigantic earthenware jars. The biggest containers always had pointed bases. They could not stand on their own, but were designed to be placed in wicker or wooden stands, The stands protected the heavy jars from breakage when they were placed on stone floors.

Anecdotes

ut True!

● COUNTING THE ENEMY DEAD

After a battle, the soldiers cut off a hand, or a nose, or some other part from each enemy corpse. The grisly tokens were thrown on a pile to await the arrival of the royal scribe who counted them.

● A CURIOUS FASHION

At banquets, men and women placed a cone of perfumed grease on their heads. During the evening, it melted slowly into the wigs that they wore, giving off pleasant scents.

Mega-infos

The Great Rameses II

Eleven Pharaohs of the New Kingdom were called Rameses. But with a reign of 67 years, and over 100 children, Rameses II was the most celebrated of all.

■ A Cunning Pharaoh

Rameses II created a great piece of propaganda when he had the walls of his temples engraved with the records of his "great victory" over the powerful Hittites of Asia Minor at the battle of Kadesh. In reality, the battle was a draw—but everyone believed Rameses was a great conqueror!

Mega-infos

■ A Great Builder
Rameses II ordered the construction of many palaces, colossal statues, and immense temples whose walls and enormous pillars were covered with hieroglyphs. The monuments of this Pharaoh are truly gigantic! After his inconclusive military expeditions, Rameses became a diplomat later in his reign. But his continual building programs drained the royal treasuries.

■ The Lives of the Poor
Not far from the splendid palaces and the magnificent temples lived ordinary Egyptians, crowded in tiny, miserable hovels. As always, they ate bread, onions, vegetables, and sometimes fish. Under the blazing sun, they worked unceasingly for the comfort and glory of Pharaoh.

■ A New City for the Rich
In the north of the country, Rameses II founded a new capital: Pi-Rameses. Surrounded by a high wall, its gates protected by carved granite *sphinxes*, the new capital held many treasures. In the center was the royal palace, glowing with gold, lapis-lazuli, and turquoise. With its shade trees, the scent of its flowers, and the orchards weighed down with fruit, life in Pi-Ramses was sweet for Pharaoh and his court.

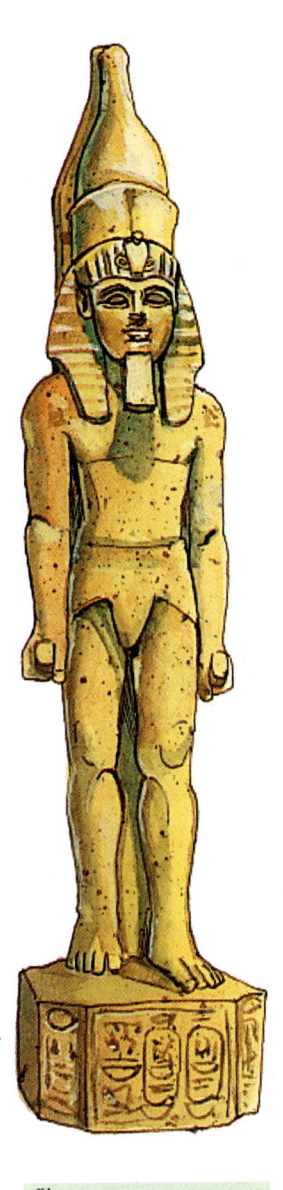

With the body of a lion and the head of a man, a sphinx was considered a divine guardian.

Mega-infos

A Village of Gifted Artisans

The specialized artisans who worked on royal tombs were not like other Egyptians.

■ Treasured Artisans

These men carried the heavy responsibility of preparing the resting places where the nobles would begin their lives in the next world. In the New Kingdom, the artisans lived in their own village in the desert near Thebes. Narrow houses made of crude bricks, one great street, and bustling workshops—that was their universe.

■ Protected or Imprisoned?

Carpenters, sculptors, painters, laborers—all were crowded together with their families in this village. High walls protected them from the dangers of the desert—prowlers, wild animals, and ghosts. But the same walls also imprisoned them. Because they knew so many secrets and worked in precious materials, it was necessary to watch them closely.

There were few undecorated places in the royal tombs. The walls were covered with images of the Gods, of Pharaoh and his queen, scenes of life on Earth or in the hereafter, and long hieroglyphic texts.

■ Artists of Great Worth

Some men hollowed out the rock. Others carried stones and earth in simple baskets. Plasterers smoothed the walls before the draftsmen arrived to trace, according to precise rules, outlines for the paintings. Master artisans supervised the work, making corrections if necessary. Then the painters applied their bright colors. The decoration of a royal tomb required many years of work.

Game

The Artisans at Work

Everyone is busy. But do you see anything strange? If you look carefully, you should be able to find twenty *anachronisms* — things unknown in ancient Egypt, that belong to another time and place.

Answers on p. 63

Game

The Learned Scientists

The scientists of ancient Egypt were masters of measurement. The Great Pyramid is laid out in a precise north-south position, with an error of only a few inches between the sides.

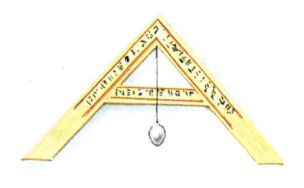

A plumb square.

■ What Was Their Secret?

Egyptian scientists created the mathematics necessary to build gigantic monuments, measure the land, calculate taxes, and track the movements of the planets and stars. With simple instruments such as the plumb line, the set square, and the compass, they built to last!

Mega-infos

■ The Astronomers

Excellent observers, the sages studied the heavens, watching the phases of the moon, the height of the sun's path, the movements of the planets and constellations. They awaited the reappearance of the star Sirius, heralding the start of the annual flooding of the Nile. Their year was made up of 12 months, but each month had only 30 days. The five extra days made a holiday at the end of the year.

■ The Doctors

Illnesses were blamed on evil spirits, so doctors were also priests or magicians. Protective charms, called *amulets,* were used along with medicines made of all sorts of substances. Some of the ingredients were ridiculous, others were poisonous, but some of the potions were excellent. Kohl, used as a kind of eyeshadow, actually protected the eyes from various ailments. The doctors also set bones and used a kind of cement to seal dental cavities.

Magical amulets.

Mega-infos

A Strange Era

After the fall of the last Rameses, about 1095 B.C., Egypt was divided. In the north, the military took power, and in the south, the priests. Troubles multiplied.

■ The Libyans Take Charge

Over several centuries, migrants from Libya filtered into Egypt. They settled peacefully and adopted Egyptian gods and customs. Little by little, they gained in importance. About 950 B.C. one of them, Sheshonk I, took power. This strong Pharaoh, who captured Jerusalem, is mentioned in the Bible. But after Sheshonk, disorder returned. Two centuries later, there were four kingdoms and numerous smaller states.

Mega-infos

■ Behold the Nubians!

Around 720 B.C., Piankhy I, the king of *Kush*❦, conquered all of Egypt. His realm stretched 1,500 miles (about 2,000 kilometers) to the Mediterranean Sea! But he was not the all-powerful god-king of former times. Instead, he was the ruler of a group of powerful states. Peace did not last long. In 664 B.C., the Asian Assyrians burst over the countryside and sacked Thebes.

❦*Kush*
Nubia, in northern Sudan.

■ Pharaoh Returns

A few years later, the Assyrian troops departed with their booty to deal with troubles at home. The Egyptians took over their land again. From his capital at Sais, Psamtik I, the greatest Pharaoh of the last native Egyptian dynasty, ruled in peace. But these were dangerous times, and these Pharaohs were constantly on the alert against foreign invasion.

The Ptolemaic temple at Edfu.

The Persians and Greeks

The arrival of the Persians marked the end of Egyptian independence. For centuries to come, the land would be ruled by foreigners.

The lighthouse of Alexandria.

Mega-infos

■ Beware the Persians!
In 525 B.C., the armies of the Persians invaded from Asia. Armed with lances and mounted on horses, the Persian cavalry destroyed the clumsy Egyptian chariots. After a single year of combat, Egypt was conquered and became part of the Persian Empire.

■ Alexander the Great
During the Persian period, many Greeks were living in Egypt, trading, teaching, and serving as soldiers. They were there to welcome Alexander the Great, son and successor to king Philip II of Macedonia, when he defeated the Persians in 332 B.C. Alexander loved Egypt. He reestablished the old religion and the old laws.

Alexander the Great.

■ Alexandria
The young conqueror built a new port beside the Mediterranean Sea. Like all the many cities he founded, he named it after himself. Alexandria soon became famous for its grandeur and culture.

■ The Good Life under the Ptolemies
After the death of Alexander in 323 B.C., his generals fought each other for control of his empire. Egypt went to Ptolemy, one of his faithful companions. This new Pharaoh and his early successors were energetic kings. Adopting many of the styles and beliefs of their Egyptian subjects, the Greeks formed the nobility and upper classes. The country became powerful and prosperous once again.

Mega-infos

End of Pharaohs

Egypt bloomed under Greek rule. But far away, at the other end of the Mediterranean Sea, the power of Rome was growing.

Octavian, the Roman emperor.

■ Rome Awaits Its Moment

The later Ptolemies disputed the throne among themselves. Their plots and quarrels weakened Egypt. Rome, having expanded around the northern Mediterranean coast, had come to the Egyptian border. Invited in by Ptolemy XI, who was trying to regain his throne, the Romans bided their time.

■ Courageous Cleopatra

About 50 B.C. Cleopatra VII, the last ruler of the Ptolemaic dynasty, tried desperately to preserve the independence of her country. But she backed the wrong side in the Roman civil war. In 31 B.C. her navy was destroyed at the battle of Actium by Octavian, the future Roman emperor Augustus. Her cause lost, Cleopatra committed suicide.

Mega-infos

■ Total Defeat

Egypt had been the last independent land along the Mediterranean Coast. With its capture, the Roman Empire was complete. There were no more Pharaohs. Not even a province of the empire, Egypt was considered the private property of the emperor, to dispose of as he wished.

The death of Cleopatra.

Quiz

True or

■ The Pharaohs loved to ride their horses in the desert.

False. The horse was unknown during the Old and Middle Kingdoms, and was only used to pull war chariots during the New Kingdom.

■ The god Amen was often depicted as a ram with a solar disk between its horns.

True.

■ Egypt has always been governed by an Egyptian Pharaoh.

False. There were many foreign Pharaohs: Hyksos, Libyans, Nubians, Greeks, and others.

■ Royal artisans could come and go as they pleased.

False. Royal artisans were closely guarded, lest they reveal secrets of the pharaoh's palace and tomb.

■ Ramses II achieved a brilliant military victory at Kadesh in Asia Minor.

False. Although his troops were not defeated, they never managed to capture the city of Kadesh.

False?

Quiz

■ **If Pharaoh had a decayed tooth, his doctor had an effective treatment.**

True. The royal doctor could seal the tooth with a mineral cement.

■ **The decorations on tombs could be completed in less than a year.**

False. These decorations sometimes required decades to complete.

■ **Alexander the Great was the son of King Philip II of Macedonia.**

True.

■ **The Roman general Octavian killed Queen Cleopatra.**

False. Cleopatra killed herself by letting a snake bite her after her fleet was destroyed by Octavian at the battle of Actium.

59

Quiz
True or

■ **The Egyptians liked locusts.**

■ **Egyptian sages invented our calendar.**

True.

■ **The Egyptians painted their eyes for medical reasons.**

True. They used kohl, a black powder mixed with oil. It protected the eyes from many diseases.

■ **Alexander the Great stayed in Egypt for a long time.**

False. He only stayed a few months before he set off to make further conquests.

False. They dreaded them. A swarm of locusts could devour a harvest in a few hours. (The Egyptians *did* like to eat locusts, which they considered a delicacy!)

60

False?

Quiz

■ **Memphis was the only capital of Egypt.**

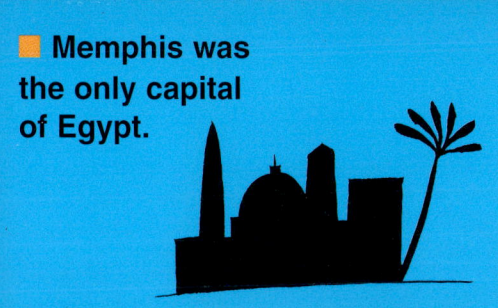

False. Memphis, Thebes, Pi-Rameses, and others were all capitals at different times.

■ **The Egyptian alphabet was very difficult to learn.**

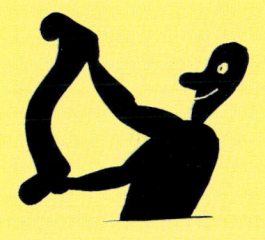

False. This is a trick question! The Egyptians did not have an alphabet. Instead, there were some 700 signs during the Old Kingdom and thousands during the Ptolemaic period.

■ **The Egyptians liked to be overweight.**

True. Being overweight was a sign of wealth.

■ **The great pyramids date from the last Pharaohs.**

False. They date from the Old Kingdom.

61

Index

Actium, 56
Ahmose, 40, 41
Alexander the Great, 13, 55
Alexandria, 55
Amenemhet, 28, 29
Amenhotep, 13
Amulet, 51
Artisans, 13, 42, 46, 47
Assyrians, 53

Barge, 22, 25, 37
Boat, 14, 19, 21, 24, 25, 28, 37

Chariot, 38, 54
Cleopatra, 13, 57

Doctor, 16, 51, 59

Fish, 36, 37, 45

Gods, 17, 21, 27, 29, 33, 36, 53
Greeks, 13, 54, 55, 56

Hieratic, 15
Hhieroglyphic, 14, 15, 45, 47
Horse, 38, 39, 54
Hyksos, 38, 39, 40

Imhotep, 16

Jerusalem, 52

Kadesh, 44
Kingdom
  Middle, 12, 18, 29, 31, 39
  New, 13, 18, 40, 41
  Old, 12, 14, 24, 26, 27, 28

Libyans, 28, 53

Magic, 31, 51
Medicine, 51
Memphis, 13
Mentuhotep, 13, 28
Mummy, 20, 21

Nile, 12, 13, 19, 29, 32, 51, 57
Nubians, 28, 52

Octavian, 57
Offering, 21, 33, 41

Papyrus, 14, 24, 36
Peasants, 13, 32, 33, 37, 38
Pepi, 12, 26
Persians, 54, 55
Pharaoh, 13, 16, 17, 19, 20, 21, 22, 24, 25, 26, 27, 28, 29, 30, 31, 32, 36, 37, 38, 39, 41, 42, 44, 46, 47, 52, 53, 55, 56, 57, 58, 59
Piankhy, 53
Pi-Rameses, 45

Plow, 34, 38
Priest, 13, 16, 31, 32, 52
Prince, 14, 26, 27, 40
Psamtik I, 53
Ptolemy, 55, 56
Pyramid, 14, 17, 20, 21, 41, 50

Rameses, 44, 45
Rome, 56, 57

Sarcophagus, 21
Scientist, 50, 51
Scribe, 13, 14, 15, 26, 32, 33, 37, 39
Senroset, 13, 28, 30
Serpent, 13, 17, 30
Shadouf, 33
Sheshonk, 52
Soldiers, 13, 43, 55

Tax, 16, 39
Temple, 14, 21, 27, 41, 44, 45, 55
Thebes, 13, 27, 28, 41, 44, 55
Thutmosis, 12, 41
Tomb, 12, 27, 41
Tutankhamen, 41

Uraeus, 30

Valley of the Kings, 13, 41
Vizier, 16

War, 38, 57
Warrior, 30, 40
Workers, 18, 19, 41

Zoser, 12, 16, 17

Answers to the puzzle on pages 48–49.

should have found: 1. a camel caravan (Roman period), 2. an electronic scale (20th century), 3. a gun (Middle ...s), 4. a propeller (France, 1827), 5. a Mayan temple (Central America, fourth century A.D.), 6. a modern ...itbrush, 7. a paint roller, 8. a modern sculpture, 9. a corkscrew (seventeenth century), 10. a large, flat-based ... jar (the Egyptians made large oil and wine jars with pointed bases), 11. a cement mixer (1925), 12. a folding ...r (1620), 13. a wineglass (glass was already in use at this time, but only as decorative beads, marbles, etc.), ...sandpaper (invented by George Washington Carver, twentieth century), 15. the Eiffel Tower (1889), 16. a pen ...ddle Ages; the Egyptian scribes wrote with brushes), 17. paper envelopes, 18. a shirt and tie, 19. a stick of ...amite (1866), 20. a block and tackle (Greece, 4th century B.C.).

Answer to the activity on pages 23–24.

...omplete the construction, place the square sides next to each other. (Note that this pyramid lacks a point.)

Photo credits for stickers
© J. P. Stevens/Ancient Art and Architecture Collection; Werner Forman Archive; © R. Sheridan/Ancient Art and Architecture Collection; Bridgeman Art Library; E. Lessing/AKG Photo; © Pete Clayton; Werner Forman Archive; © Brooklyn Museum of Art; E. Lessing/AKG Photo; Robert Harding Associates; Werner Forman Archive; © British Museum; © Pete Clayton; © M. Jelliffe/Ancient Art and Architecture Collection.

Photo credits for picture cards (left to right)
Top: Bridgeman Art Library; © The Griffith Institute/Ashmolean Museum, Oxford; © M. Jelliffe/Ancient Art and Architecture Collection; © Pete Clayton; © Zefa-First; © M. Jelliffe/Ancient Art and Architecture Collection.
Bottom: © Pete Clayton; Giraudon/Bridgeman Art Library; Werner Forman Archive; Giraudon/Bridgeman Art Library; © P. Oxford/Natural History Unit; Werner Forman Archive/Egyptian Museum, Cairo.

Illustrations
Ian Chamberlain, Peter Dennis, Francesca D'Ottavi, Jeff Fisher, Chris Forsey,
Lynda Grey, Daniel Guerrier, Nicki Palin

© 1997 by Editions Nathan, Paris, France
The title of the French edition is *Fascinants pharaons d'Egypte*
Published by Les Editions Nathan, Paris.

English translation © Copyright 1998 by Nathan LaRousse PLC

Barron's edition adapted by Robert Reis.

All rights reserved.
No part of this book may be reproduced in any form, by photostat, microfilm, xerography, or any other means, or incorporated into any information retrieval system, electronic or mechanical, without the written permission of the copyright owner.

All inquiries should be addressed to:
Barron's Educational Series, Inc.
250 Wireless Boulevard
Hauppauge, New York 11788

Library of Congress Catalog Card No. 97-77436

International Standard Book No. 0-7641-5096-0

Printed in Italy
9 8 7 6 5 4 3 2 1

Stickers

Mummy of Rameses II

Cleopatra, gold coin

Protective amulet

Papyrus

A seated scribe, 18th dynasty

Cartouche (a person's name)

Mentuhotep

Alexander the Great and his horse Bukephalus

Stickers

Pepi I

Khufu

Gold mask of Tutankhamen

Small model of a sailing boat

Small model of a granary

Ahmose

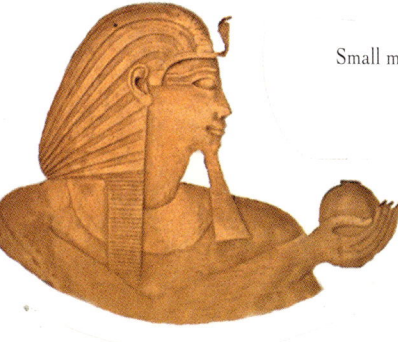

Senroset

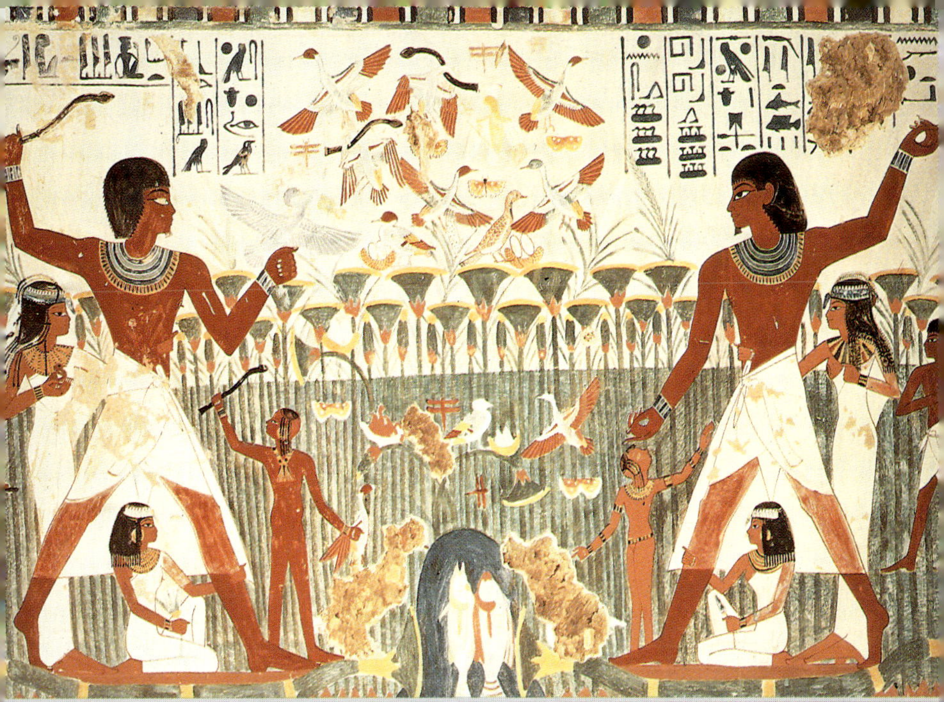
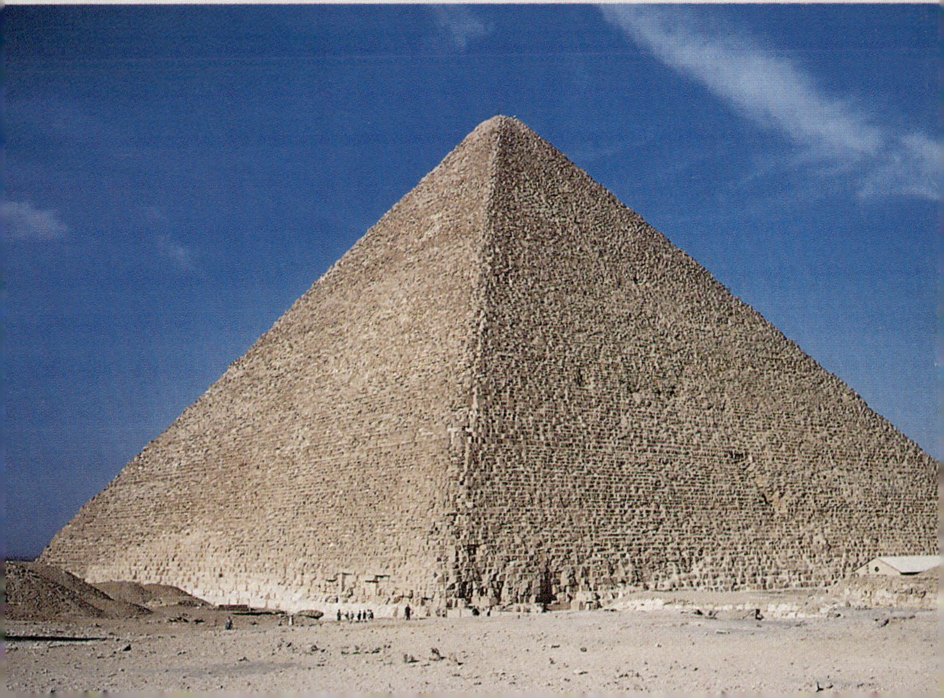

Picture Cards

Hunting

Hunting wild ducks or catching fish in the marshes was a pleasant pastime for noble Egyptians. Standing on his papyrus boat, accompanied by his family, the prince hits birds with a throwing stick. His young son imitates him.

(Tomb of Prince Nakht, 1410 B.C., Thebes.)

Picture Cards

Khufu's Pyramid

Khufu's pyramid, formerly 480 feet (147 meters) tall, has lost its point, and measures only 450 feet (137 meters). In this amazing tomb, the interior corridors and rooms have no inscriptions. Inside the "King's chamber" there is only the royal sarcophagus, made of granite.

Picture Cards

The Double Crown

The double crown, also called *pshent*, was made up of the red crown of Lower Egypt on top of the white crown of Upper Egypt. It symbolized the unity of the country, ruled by one Pharaoh.

Picture Cards

The Sarcophagus of Tutankhamen

In the Valley of the Kings, Howard Carter started the searches that led to the discovery of the tomb of Tutankhamen in 1922. He found a small tomb, modest for a Pharaoh, but almost intact.

Picture Cards

Soldier on a Chariot

In the New Kingdom, the Egyptians used horses and chariots: light carts on which stood a driver and a fighter. Horses were precious animals, available only to Pharaoh and the nobles.

Picture Cards

The Pharaoh's Name

Proper names were symbolically tied up with string in a *cartouche*, separating the name from the rest of the text. Pharaohs had separate names for Lower and Upper Egypt, thus the two cartouches.

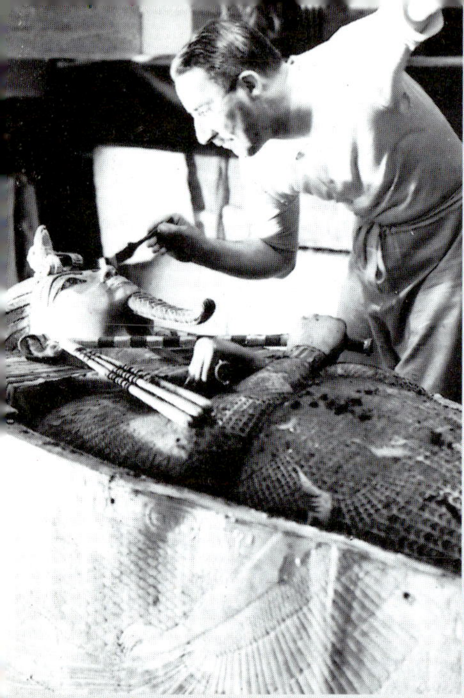
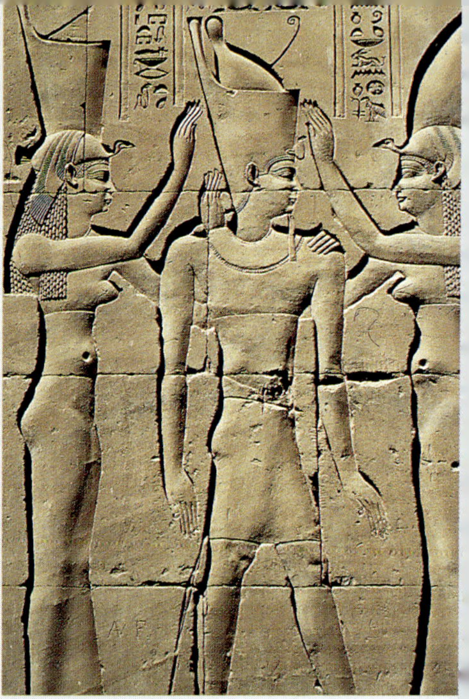
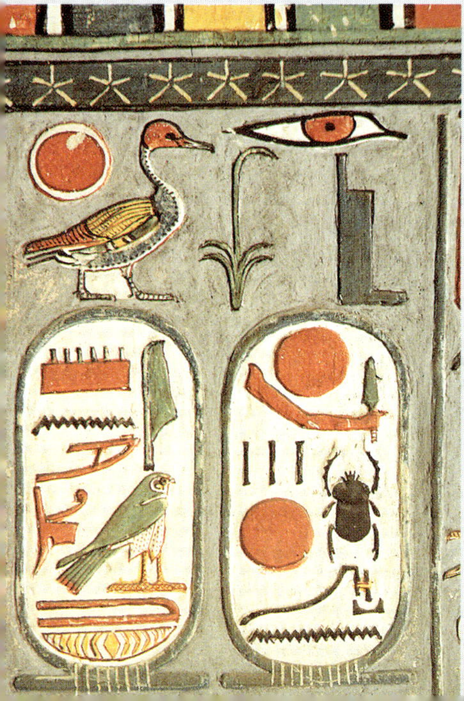
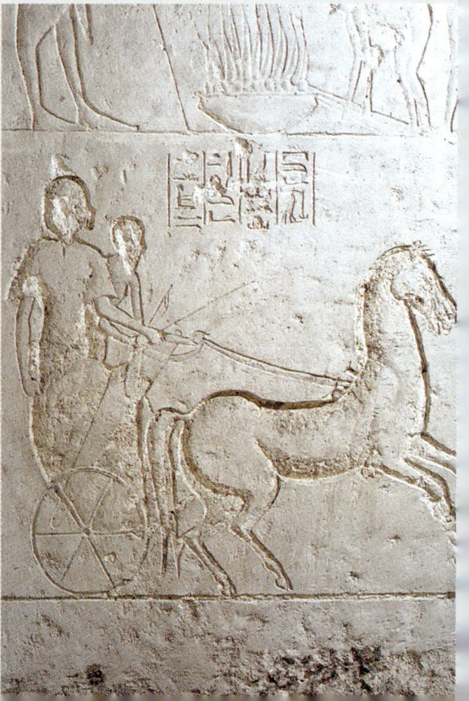

Picture Cards

Sennedjem, the Workman

Sennedjem and his wife work in the fields in the afterlife, just as they did on Earth. Pulled by oxen, his plow digs into the soft ground. Sycamores and date palms grow nearby.

Picture Cards

Pharaoh's Pikemen

Armed with long-pointed pikes, protected by shields covered with cowhides, barefoot, and dressed in a simple loincloth, these pikemen parade or leave to fight in places far away for the greater glory of Pharaoh.

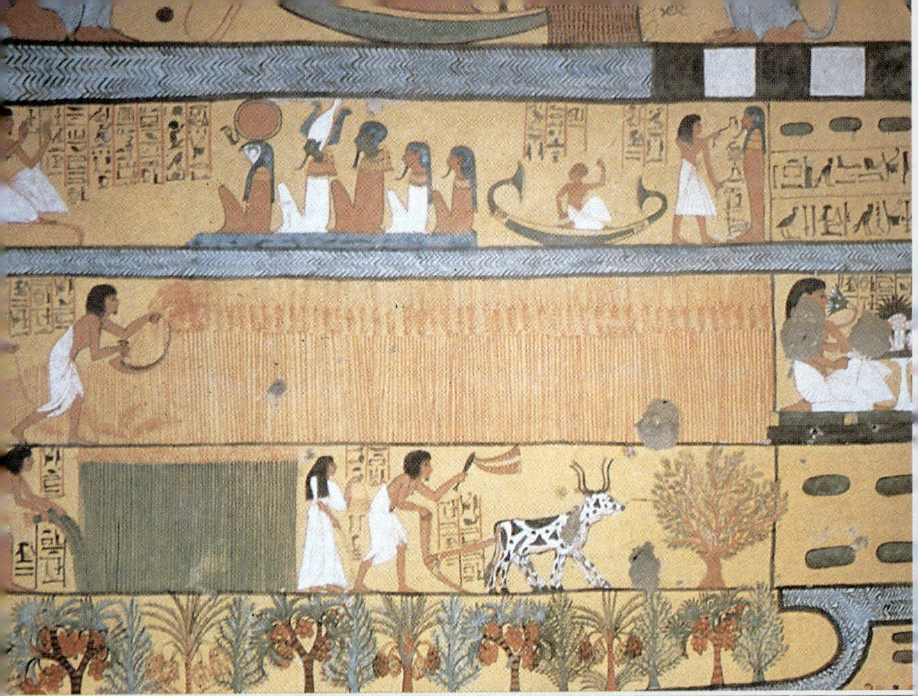

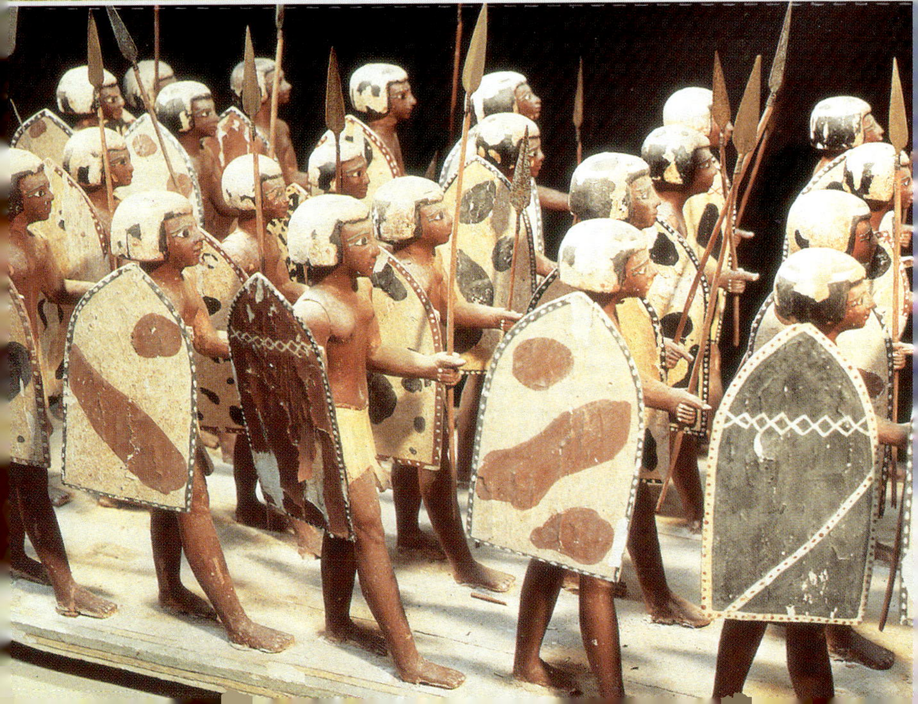

Picture Cards

The Temple of Abu Simbel

This gigantic temple, carved in the rocks for Rameses II and decorated with four colossal statues, was moved recently to save it from the rising waters behind the Aswan High Dam.

Picture Cards

Zoser's Pyramid

Almost 5,000 years old, built by the architect Imhotep, the step pyramid was surrounded by numerous buildings, among them curious "false temples."

Picture Cards

Carving of a Marsh Scene

The papyrus reeds sheltered numerous animals and had many uses. The stems were bundled to make boats, or were woven into mats, baskets, or sandals, and the fibrous core was made into paper-like sheets for writing.

Picture Cards

Papyrus Plants

Thick stands of papyrus grew in the marshes of ancient Egypt. With its tall stems topped by fine tassels, the plants can reach about 20 feet (6 meters) in height!

Titles in the Megascope series:

Amazing Nature

Searching for Human Origins

Understanding the Human Body

Life in the Middle Ages

Mysteries, True and False

The Pharaohs of Ancient Egypt

BARRON'S

Barron's Educational Series, Inc.
250 Wireless Blvd., Hauppauge, NY 11788